Piano Practice Notebook

Dear student,

now you need never forget w
you during your music lesson. Just take this book with
you to note down everything you need to work on at
.home.

There are a few pages of blank manuscript paper at the
back of the book so that you can make a note of any
tunes, scales or key signatures you need to remember.
Or maybe you would like to write your own short
composition ready show to your teacher at the next
lesson.

There is also a small guide to music theory, in case you
forget any of the basics.

If you are preparing for an exam you can use the scale
chart to keep track of which scales and arpeggios you
have so far learnt.

Good luck with your music practice, and don't forget to
take your notebook with you to every lesson!

Lesson date:

Scales and exercises:

Pieces:

Other work:

This week's tip: *try to practise a little every day.*

Lesson date:

Scales and exercises:

Pieces:

Other work:

This week's tip: *practise slowly before you try to play quickly.*

Lesson date:

Scales and exercises:

Pieces:

Other work:

This week's tip: *practise the difficult bars in the music more than the rest.*

Lesson date:

Scales and exercises:

Pieces:

Other work:

This week's tip: *count out difficult bars and clap the rhythm before you play.*

Lesson date:

Scales and exercises:

Pieces:

Other work:

This week's tip: *if you find reading the notes difficult, try to name them before playing them.*

Lesson date:

Scales and exercises:

Pieces:

Other work:

This week's tip: *if there are words, sing the tune before you play it.*

Lesson date

Scales and exercises:

Pieces:

Other work:

This week's tip: *if there are no words, make some up, then sing the song!*

Lesson date

Scales and exercises:

Pieces:

Other work:

This week's tip: *check that you are using the correct fingering for every note.*

Lesson date

Scales and exercises:

Pieces:

Other work:

This week's tip: *be careful to play the correct rhythms.*

Lesson date

Scales and exercises:

Pieces:

Other work:

This week's tip: *read the music carefully and check you are playing loud and quiet at the correct places.*

Lesson date

Scales and exercises:

Pieces:

Other work:

This week's tip: *check your posture.*

Lesson date

Scales and exercises:

Pieces:

Other work:

This week's tip: *if you can play a piece well, why not play it to family and/or friends?*

Lesson date

Scales and exercises:

Pieces:

Other work:

This week's tip: *aim to sight read at least one piece each week.*

Lesson date

Scales and exercises:

Pieces:

Other work:

This week's tip: *sometimes, when you play through a piece or a scale, give yourself a mark out of 10!*

Lesson date

Scales and exercises:

Pieces:

Other work:

This week's tip: *try to memorise the difficult bits of the music.*

Lesson date

Scales and exercises:

Pieces:

Other work:

This week's tip: *when practising scales, arpeggios or broken chords, make sure that they are at the same speed throughout.*

Lesson date

Scales and exercises:

Pieces:

Other work:

This week's tip: *learn what a chromatic scale is and how to play it.*

Lesson date

Scales and exercises:

Pieces:

Other work:

This week's tip: *sometimes play everything as quietly as you can.*

Lesson date

Scales and exercises:

Pieces:

Other work:

This week's tip: *sometimes play everything as loud as you can.*

Lesson date

Scales and exercises:

Pieces:

Other work:

This week's tip: *if you find it difficult to find time to do enough practice, make sure that you at least do some on the day before your lesson.*

Lesson date

Scales and exercises:

Pieces:

Other work:

This week's tip: *the golden rule with sight reading is "play slowly but keep going".*

Lesson date

Scales and exercises:

Pieces:

Other work:

This week's tip: *when you are sight reading, don't forget to check the key signature.*

Lesson date

Scales and exercises:

Pieces:

Other work:

This week's tip: *start your practice with scales or technical exercises to warm up your fingers.*

Lesson date

Scales and exercises:

Pieces:

Other work:

This week's tip: *find a piece you learnt previously and play it again.*

Lesson date

Scales and exercises:

Pieces:

Other work:

This week's tip: *practise the first four bars of your piece more than the rest: you want to make a good start.*

Lesson date

Scales and exercises:

Pieces:

Other work:

This week's tip: *if you can play your scales well, start to play them faster.*

Lesson date

Scales and exercises:

Pieces:

Other work:

This week's tip: *pay special attention to the last few bars of your pieces, you want to finish well and leave a good impression!*

Lesson date

Scales and exercises:

Pieces:

Other work:

This week's tip: *think of a piece of music you like and know well and try to play it by ear.*

Lesson date

Scales and exercises:

Pieces:

Other work:

This week's tip: *once you can play a piece fairly well, try to make up an alternative ending for it.*

Lesson date

Scales and exercises:

Pieces:

Other work:

This week's tip: *can you compose a short introduction to your favourite piece?*

Lesson date

Scales and exercises:

Pieces:

Other work:

This week's tip: *ask your teacher to play to you one of his or her own favourite pieces.*

Lesson date

Scales and exercises:

Pieces:

Other work:

This week's tip: *sometimes play your scales staccato.*

Lesson date

Scales and exercises:

Pieces:

Other work:

This week's tip: *memorise the italian terms at the back of this book!*

Lesson date

Scales and exercises:

Pieces:

Other work:

This week's tip: *try to play the right hand (treble clef) part of one of your pieces with the left hand.*

Lesson date

Scales and exercises:

Pieces:

Other work:

This week's tip: *watch someone playing the piano on youtube.*

Lesson date

Scales and exercises:

Pieces:

Other work:

This week's tip: *learn how to play the chords of C major and G major.*

Basic Music Theory

 This is a treble clef.

In piano music the right hand plays the treble clef notes.

𝄢 This is a bass clef.

In piano music the left hand plays the bass clef notes.

Note values:

𝅝 = semibreve - 4 beats

𝅗𝅥 = minim - 2 beats

♩ = crotchet -1 beat

♪ = quaver - ½ beat

♬ = semiquaver - ¼ beat

Time signatures:

Simple time:

2/4 two crotchet beats per bar

3/4 three crotchet beats per bar

4/4 four crotchet beats per bar

Compound time:

6/8 two dotted crotchet beats per bar

9/8 three dotted crotchet beats per bar

12/8 four dotted crotchet beats per bar

Common Italian terms:

p *(piano)* = quiet

f *(forte)* = loud

mp *(mezzo piano)* = moderately quiet

mf *(mezzo forte)* = moderately loud

pp *(pianissimo)* = very quiet

ff *(fortissimo)* = very loud

cresc. = gradually get louder

dim. = gradually get quieter

allegro = quick

andante = at a medium speed

lento = slow

presto = very fast

Note names:

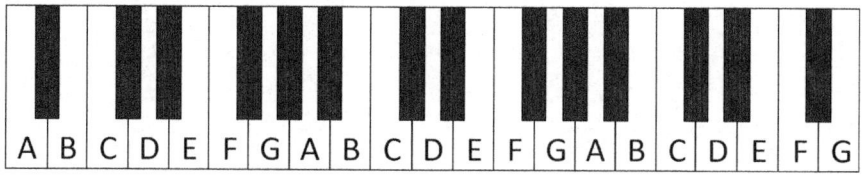

Accidentals:

♯ = a sharp, raises the note that follows by a semitone

♭ = a flat, lowers the note that follows by a semitone

♮ = a natural, cancels a sharp or flat

Key signatures:

Scale Chart

This list shows most of the common scales and arpeggios that you need to know in grades 1, 2 and 3. Tick the box once you know a scale or arpeggio so that you can keep track of what you have done. (If you are taking grade one you will learn broken chords instead of arpeggios).

	scales			arpeggios		
	left hand	right hand	hands together	left hand	right hand	hands together
C major						
G major						
D major						
A major						
E major						
B major						
F major						
B♭ major						
E♭ major						
A♭ major						
A minor						
E minor						
B minor						
F♯ minor						
C♯ minor						
D minor						
G minor						
C minor						
F minor						

Printed in Great Britain
by Amazon